ISBN 978-0-692-80588-6

Printed in Minneapolis, MN, USA

N

W

E

From Eat Street, with Love

STORIES & RECIPES FROM MINNEAPOLIS' BEST TASTING NEIGHBORHOOD

S

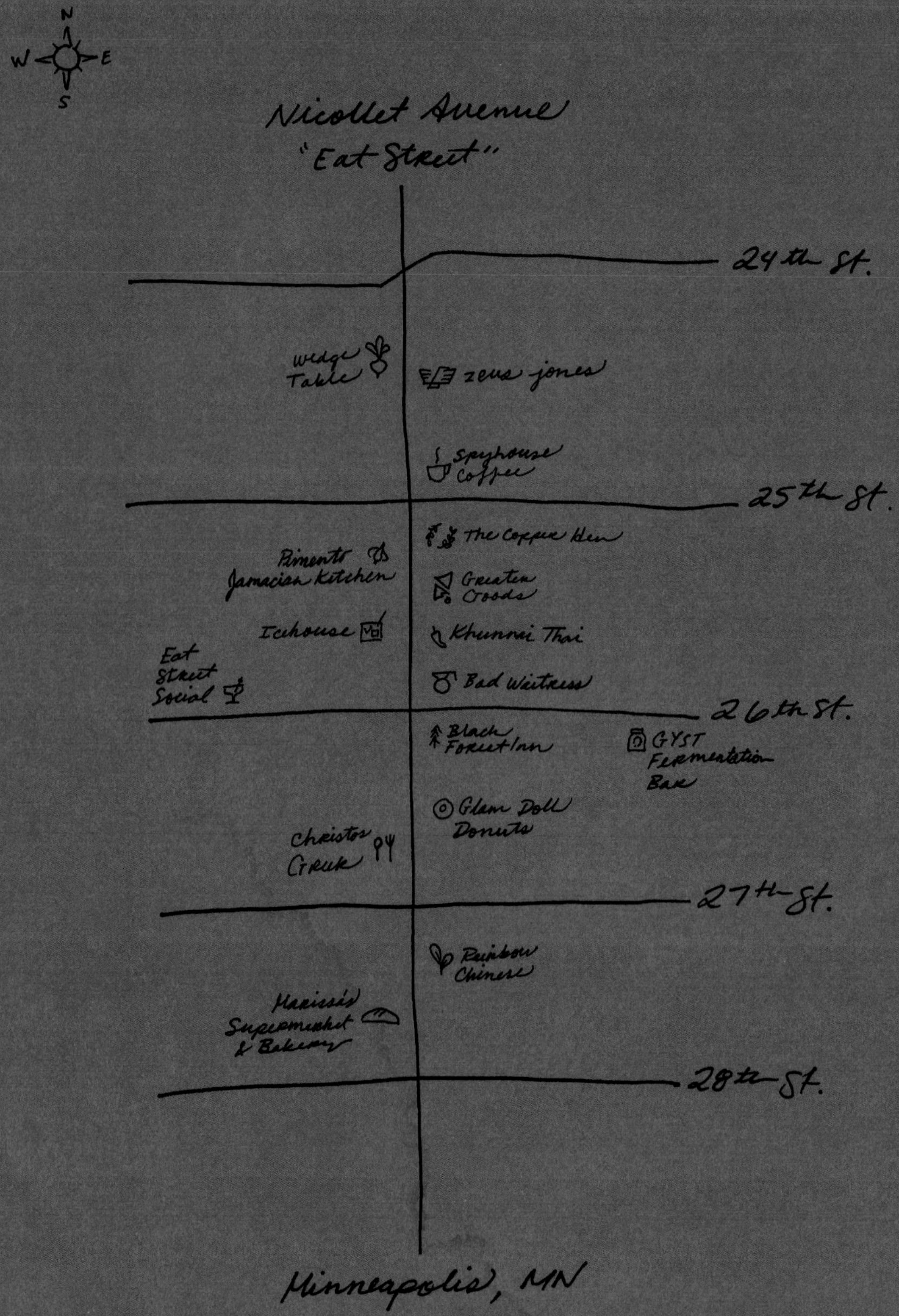
N
W
E
S
Nicollet Avenue
"Eat Street"
24th St.
Wedge Table
zeus jones
Spyhouse Coffee
25th St.
The Copper Hen
Pimento Jamacian Kitchen
Greater Goods
Icehouse
Khunnai Thai
Eat Street Social
Bad Waitress
26th St.
Black Forest Inn
GYST Fermentation Bar
Glam Doll Donuts
Christos Greek
27th St.
Rainbow Chinese
Marissa's Supermarket & Bakery
28th St.
Minneapolis, MN

Introduction

What you're about to read is a cookbook that only scratches the surface of one of the most flavorful neighborhoods in the Midwest. "Eat Street" — as we call it here in Minneapolis — is a unique stretch of 17 blocks on the south side of Nicollet Avenue. Like a culinary mini United Nations, it has managed to attract and retain unique restaurants and business owners from all over the world.

The uniqueness of dishes is only the beginning of what makes Eat Street different. One of the first things we noticed in creating this cookbook was how welcoming and open the neighborhood truly is. Instead of being guarded about their personal stories and sought-after recipes, many embraced the opportunity to share them with everyone. This good will and collaboration extended beyond recipes — our interviews revealed stories of Eat Street business owners helping one another and a real respect (and craving) for one another's dishes.

That's why we wanted to bring these dishes to you. As new members of the Eat Street business community, we are truly humbled by the amazing food and inspiring people this neighborhood has to offer. Our admiration doesn't stop at lunchtime; we've had the fortune of working with many food companies as clients over the years and Eat Street's creativity and entrepreneurial spirit continue to inspire and motivate us.

IN AN EFFORT TO GIVE BACK AND KEEP THE NEIGHBORHOOD STRONG, WE ARE DONATING ALL PROCEEDS TO THE WHITTIER ALLIANCE.

We hope you enjoy bringing Eat Street into your home!

Zeus Jones
2429 Nicollet Avenue
www.zeusjones.com

Table of Contents

Treats

2
1

Starters, Sides, and Salads

Pimento Jamaican Kitchen

2524 Nicollet Avenue

Sometimes, a restaurant comes along that fills a familiar niche in a totally unexpected way. Pimento Jamaican Kitchen, with its Caribbean comfort food, is that restaurant. Whether you're digging into one of their coconut rice bowls, piled high with jerk chicken and sweet plantains, or a warm and filling Jamaican hand pie, you won't leave hungry.

The fact that Pimento offers unique flavors built on a winning template is no accident. The original location, opened by Tomme Vevvas and Yoni Reinharz in the nearby suburb of Burnsville about three years ago, was the winner of the Food Network's Food Court Wars. And the idea that was so solid that it was worth a reality TV championship has also proven worthy of success both in the suburbs and on Eat Street.

Tomme was born and raised in Kingston, Jamaica, and learned to cook from his grandmother; her recipes are used throughout Pimento's menu. Ten years ago, Tomme moved to Minneapolis to take a job with a large corporation, doing community development programs all over the globe. Tomme and Yoni happened to be neighbors, and eventually realized they both had a common love: food.

"I'M THE GUY WHO'S MAKING JAMAICAN LIFE ACCESSIBLE TO MINNESOTANS! THAT'S PRETTY AWESOME."

"I tried Tomme's food and got hooked," says Yoni. "I pitched him the idea of starting a food truck, to see if he could help develop the menu. I never dreamt he'd leave his fancy job to come sell chicken with me! But it turned out that he had a plan for this very business from his college days, envisioning a kind of Jamaican-style Chipotle. We got the ball rolling."

According to Yoni, the diversity of Pimento's clientele is something he values dearly. "The fact that literally anyone and everyone feels welcome here... It worked in a way I could have never guessed... I'm proud to be a steward of my community in that regard, and to be an emissary for Jamaican food and culture in a city that's very culturally aware, yet starved of that particular culture. I'm the guy who's making Jamaican life accessible to Minnesotans! That's pretty awesome."

Kill Dem Wid It! Wings

Starter

Total time: 1 hr. + 24 hr. marinade

Serves 4-6

INGREDIENTS

MARINADE

3 to 5 pounds chicken wings

1/4 cup Pimento Kill Dem Wid It! Sauce (or your favorite hot sauce)

Juice of one lime

1 inch fresh ginger

10 cloves garlic

FINISHING SAUCE

1/2 cup butter

2 tablespoons reserved marinade

Juice of 2 limes

1/4 cup soy sauce

1 habanero pepper, diced

1 teaspoon allspice

2 tablespoons lime zest

GARNISH (optional)

3 large scallions, thinly sliced

DIRECTIONS

Preparation

Blend all sauce ingredients in a blender or food processor until smooth. Reserve 2 tablespoons of the marinade for the finishing sauce. In a resealable bag or container, cover the wings with sauce, and marinate for 24 hours in the refrigerator.

Combine all finishing sauce ingredients in a blender and blend until smooth. Pour the blended mixture slowly into the bowl of melted butter, whisking as you pour. Set aside.

Assembly

After the wings have marinated, preheat the oven to 425 degrees and place an oven rack in the middle position. Prepare the finishing sauce if you haven't already done so.

Cover a baking sheet with aluminum foil and spray with cooking spray. Place wings in an even layer, skin side down. Pour half of the finishing sauce over the wings, reserving the other half.

Bake the wings for 30 minutes, then turn them over so the skin is facing up, and bake 15 to 20 minutes more.

Once they're done baking, turn on the broiler and broil the wings for 3 to 5 minutes, or until evenly browned and a bit crisp. Move the broiled wings to a bowl and toss with the remaining sauce. Garnish with scallions and enjoy!

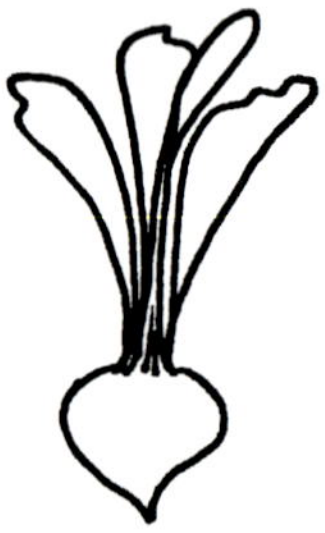

Wedge Table

2412 Nicollet Avenue

What happens when you start with kitchen space for a grocery store and add a café and to-go prepared food shop, all built around meeting your community's needs? The Wedge Table happens.

When the owners of the Wedge Co-op realized it needed space for catering operations and prepared food, they chose to open on Nicollet because of the possibilities it held for giving back to the neighborhood. Because the Wedge is member-owned and has community values woven into its charter, it sees a big opportunity as new neighbors on Eat Street to offer resources to local non-profits, businesses, and community groups, especially through its full kitchens and community rooms.

"I THINK THAT MEETING OTHER PEOPLE AROUND HERE AND DEVELOPING CAMARADERIE IS IMPORTANT."

"The Wedge has roots in this neighborhood — it started as a tiny basement co-op," says Colin Cody, Product Development Chef. "We make every decision based on what's good for the community and our values, not for growth's sake. All of our profits go back to the community."

Colin is excited about how the Wedge Table will evolve as a central community-gathering place. A recent pop-up with local bagel makers Rise Bagels was a success, and the Wedge has plans to do a donut and beer pairing event with Surly Brewing and neighboring Glam Doll Donuts.

"I think we stand out as being a peer," says Colin. "We're able to curate a local selection of goods from local vendors. That's one of the nice things about being a market — we're not driven entirely by the profit margin on our menu items. Everyone that we reach out to, we can use their product in some way. That's probably the most enjoyable part of my job, seeing what everyone else is doing."

Salad	
Total time: 30 min.	Serves 6-8

WEDGE TABLE

Grapefruit Fennel Slaw

INGREDIENTS

2 cups green cabbage, cored and shredded

1 cup red cabbage, cored and shredded

1 cup carrot, grated

1 grapefruit, cut into supremes (instructions on page 21)

1 apple (Pink Lady or Braeburn-or any other crisp, tart red apple)

1/2 bulb fresh fennel, shaved on a mandoline or sliced finely

1/2 teaspoon sea salt

3/4 ounce fresh mint, chopped fine

1/3 cup lemon vinaigrette dressing

LEMON VINAIGRETTE

Yields 2 cups

Total Time: 10 min.

Zest of one lemon

Juice of one lemon

2 tablespoons honey

1 teaspoon whole grain mustard

1 teaspoon sea salt

1 pinch black pepper

2/3 cup olive oil

2/3 cup avocado, peanut, or sunflower oil

DIRECTIONS

Lemon Vinaigrette

Combine ingredients in a jar with a secure lid and shake. The dressing itself is bright and vibrant, great with any green salad with fruit or nuts, and pairs well with blue, goat, or sheep's milk cheeses. This recipe yields 2 cups of dressing — more than you'll need for the slaw. Refrigerate the remainder and use for up to two weeks.

Grapefruit Fennel Slaw

Make supremes from the grapefruit by removing the peel and pith on the top and bottom, then setting it flat on the cutting board. Remove the peel with your knife, cutting just past the pith and following the contour of the fruit from top to bottom, one knife's width at a time. Repeat until the whole grapefruit is peeled. Now cut segments of fruit out by holding the grapefruit and cutting at an angle as close to the white walls of the segments as possible. Remove all segments and reserve the center.

Dice the apple and squeeze the reserved grapefruit center over the diced apple. Toss together with the mint. This will help prevent the apple from oxidizing and macerate the mint to help draw out more flavor.

Toss all ingredients together thoroughly. As with most slaws, the longer it sits, the more the cabbage breaks down and the flavors meld. It's great fresh and gets a little better for a day or so before it starts getting too soft.

Serve alongside barbeque, pulled pork, sausage and brats, or Pimento's *Kill Dem Wid It! Wings* (see recipe on page 15).

Christo's Greek Restaurant

2632 Nicollet Avenue

When Mediterranean hospitality and a true urban neighborhood community come together, it's a match made in heaven. Christo's, which got its start in 1988 when Carol Parpas and her husband gave up corporate life to work for themselves, brings the family values of Greece together with the vibrant community of the urban core.

"My husband is from Cypress," says Carol, "so all the recipes are family recipes — he's a Greek Cypriot. This was our first venture. It's been very exciting!"

It's been a long journey from just starting out to long-term success, but the character of Nicollet has always been an asset and a joy.

"We own the building, and we lease to a Somali daycare in the space next to us — which is something I could never have imagined 28 years ago! It's such a colorful neighborhood. We just love the urban environment. I like it better than the suburbs. The diversity and being in a denser part of the city is something that makes this restaurant and neighborhood absolutely unique."

> "THE DIVERSITY AND BEING IN A DENSER PART OF THE CITY IS SOMETHING THAT MAKES THIS RESTAURANT AND NEIGHBORHOOD ABSOLUTELY UNIQUE."

But the community around Christo's isn't limited to the businesses in the neighborhood. Customers are so central to the restaurant's identity that they've become an extended family — one close enough to come along on family vacations.

"We have a relationship with ninety percent of the people who walk through the door. Every other year, we've taken some customers to Greece on trips — a lot of the pictures on the wall are photos we've taken on these trips, and it really bonds us with our customers because they come back and see the photos and say 'Oh, do you remember when we were in Santorini or Mykonos...' so it's something we've really created for people that enjoy not only the food, but those who are really interested in the culture of Greece and Cypress."

Starter	Serves 6-8
Prep: 45 min.	
Total: 1 hr.	veggie V

CHRISTO'S GREEK RESTAURANT

Spanakopita

INGREDIENTS

1 pound fresh spinach

1/4 cup virgin olive oil

1/2 cup finely chopped yellow onion

1/2 cup finely chopped green onion

2 cloves garlic, crushed

3 tablespoons chopped fresh dill

1 cup crumbled feta cheese

1/4 cup ricotta cheese

2 eggs, lightly beaten

1/2 cup (1 stick) butter, melted

6 sheets phyllo dough

1 teaspoon salt

1/2 teaspoon pepper

INSIDER TIP

If you're working with phyllo dough at home, chances are it's coming frozen from a grocery. In that case, be sure to plan ahead — it will need to thaw in the refrigerator overnight, and may need to stand at room temperature for over an hour before using.

INSIDER TIP

Be sure not to over salt the spinach, as the feta brings plenty of saltiness to the final mixture.

DIRECTIONS

Preparation

Wash and de-stem spinach; drain thoroughly; cut into 1/4 inch lengths.

Heat the olive oil in a large skillet. Add the onions and garlic, sautéing until lightly browned and fragrant (2–3 minutes). Add the dill and spinach, and continue to sauté until all moisture has evaporated. Add salt and pepper, and season to taste.

Let the sautéed mixture cool completely. Add the eggs, feta, and ricotta; mix thoroughly by hand. Create several four-ounce balls (roughly 2 inches in diameter) out of the finished spinach mix and set aside.

Assembly

Lay one sheet of phyllo dough flat on a work surface. Brush the dough lightly with melted butter, working from the edge towards the center. Layer two more sheets of phyllo over the first, lightly buttering each one. Cut the phyllo into two halves.

Lay a ball of the mix in the center of each half, leaving two inches between the edge closest to you and the filling.

Fold the two-inch flap over the ball of filling, then fold in the sides and tightly roll the ball away from you. Brush the roll lightly with butter and place it seam-side down on an ungreased baking sheet.

Continue the process until the batch of mix is used up. Bake on a sheet pan in a 350-degree oven until golden, 20 to 25 minutes.

INSIDER TIP

Last, you may be familiar with triangular shaped spanakopita. Christos' technique is a little different in that the phyllo dough is folded and rolled around the filling in more of a burrito-like shape; halve them for a beautiful presentation.

GYST Fermentation Bar

25 E 26th Street

Walk into GYST on any given night of the week, and you'll see people eating what looks like visual art: large, obsidian-black platters with seasonal pickles, cheeses, charcuterie, and flavorful garnishes, the whole thing reminiscent of a painter's palette. This is the GYST Mother Board, and it's an encapsulation of the restaurant's mission: flavors that come together to complement the ancient art of fermentation.

GYST is dedicated to fermentation, the world's oldest food preservation method. It's a process that's both dead simple and endlessly complex — a fascinating equation of decomposition, terroir, and time. And because fermentation is unfamiliar to many people, visiting GYST can be as much an educational experience as it is a culinary one. Sisters and owners Ky and Mel Guse are intensely passionate about highlighting the love and effort that winemakers, cheese mongers and farmers all over the world put into their products.

In a way, the eclectic and complementary nature of the Mother Board and GYST's other offerings reflects the composition of the neighborhood itself, in all its complexity and harmony.

"You have this neighborhood," says Ky, "that brings in really awesome creative people from MCAD [Minneapolis College of Art & Design] and the Mia [Minneapolis Institute of Arts], and then you have this street — where you have a place like the Black Forest Inn that's 50 years old, you know? Or just all of the really different places that you can visit within four blocks."

"WE REALLY NEED TO DO OUR VERY BEST TO PRESERVE THE NEIGHBORHOOD AS IT WAS AND AS IT STOOD... WE'VE ALL FOUND THIS PLACE THAT REALLY FEELS LIKE HOME, AND IT'S IMPORTANT THAT WE ALL SUPPORT EACH OTHER."

Being a relative newcomer to Eat Street, Ky and Mel are acutely conscientious of how they hope GYST can help bolster and perpetuate the unique character of the neighborhood.

"When we think about small business models in food, or even small sustainable farms and agriculture — we really think those people have to work together," says Ky. "So I feel like it's the same way here — with GYST being part of the newer phase [of Eat Street], we really need to do our very best to preserve the neighborhood as it was and as it stood... We've all found this place that really feels like home, and it's important that we all support each other."

Old Dutch
POTATO CHIPS
SOUP
MASTERING CHEESE
BIBLE
PLENTY MORE
KITCHEN SIMPLE

GYST
Made in MPLS
GYST Fermentation Bar is a family-owned, producer-driven business. Good food comes from good people, so we highlight our favorite artisanal producers and farmers, and connect you to their products and stories.
GYST
Made in MPLS
CELERIAC
LEEK
ROSEMARY
12 oz
BEST BY 3·3·17

Starter or Side Dish	
Total: 30 min. + fermentation	Yields 2 qrts
	veggie V
Ferments for 10 - 15 days	

GYST FERMENTATION BAR

Celeriac, Leek, Rosemary Traditional Pickle

INGREDIENTS

5 pounds celeriac

1 1/2 pounds leeks

1/2 ounce rosemary leaves

Non-iodized sea salt

Kitchen scale

Like all fermentation processes, for this pickle it's crucial to start with clean materials and avoid cross contamination — boil your jar(s) and utensils and let them cool before beginning.

Weights are the key measurement in fermentation, so you will need a kitchen scale to execute this recipe properly. For each weight, be sure to put the bowl or vessel you're using on the scale first, then zero it before weighing the ingredients that you put in the bowl.

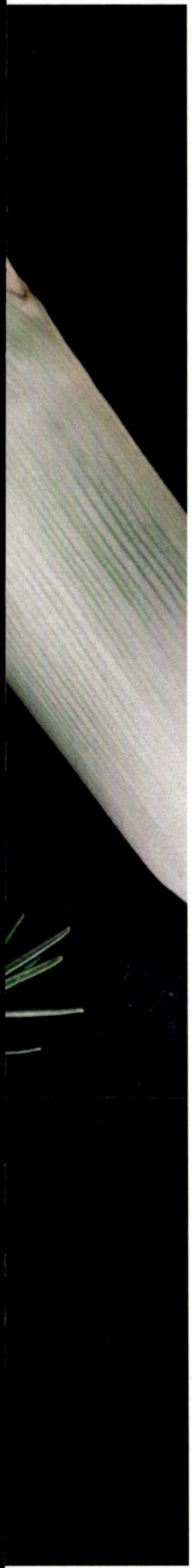

DIRECTIONS

Wash and peel the celeriac, then quarter it and slice into ¼-inch pieces. Wash and slice leeks into thin, ⅛-inch slices. Finely chop the rosemary leaves. Weigh the celeriac and leeks and set aside.

Once the cleaned and prepped vegetables have been weighed, measure 2.5% of the vegetable weight in salt (vegetable weight x 0.025) using the kitchen scale. Add the rosemary to the salt, and incorporate thoroughly with the celeriac and leeks in a large bowl.

Let the mixture sit for 2 to 4 hours, sweating the water out from the vegetables to create a brine. Pack into a non-reactive, food-safe container — a half-gallon wide-mouth Ball jar is ideal. Pack the mixture into the jar, pressing down as you go to maximize brine release and push out excess air.

Leave approximately one inch of room at top of the jar, and press down to cover the vegetables with brine. It is important that the vegetables are fully submerged in brine, as fermentation only happens in an anaerobic environment (meaning "without air").

Place a layer of plastic wrap on top of the vegetable mixture, lining the unfilled jar to prevent air or debris from getting in. Place a smaller jar, a resealable bag filled with water, or a clean, flat rock on top of the plastic to ensure the mixture stays submerged in the brine during fermentation.

Fermentation is complete in 10 to 15 days. Remove the weight and plastic wrap. Cover with a lid and keep in the refrigerator. The pickle will keep, without substantial changes in flavor, for up to six months.

Black Forest Inn

1 E 26th Street

With roots that run 51 years deep, the Black Forest Inn is an Eat Street institution. But the Chryst family — Erich, his wife Joanne, and their daughter Erica — who have owned and operated the Black Forest since 1965, don't spend too much time reflecting on their status as a destination for everyone from locals to famous celebrities. They simply get down to the everyday work of running a great restaurant, as they have for decades.

The Eat Street neighborhood has been essential to the longevity of the Black Forest Inn. When it first opened its doors, it was supported by some of the same neighbors as today — mostly students and staff from the nearby Mia, Children's Theater, and MCAD. "The artists are way up first on the list. At least in the early years, we got a lot of advice and help," Joanne says. "That community was very kind, reliable." The artistic crowd not only produced some of the iconic photographs that hang in the bar, but some colorful stories as well — a framed print of Richard Avedon's "Daughters of the American Revolution," complete with a series of bullet holes from a fateful night decades ago, is a must-see artifact for visitors.

"WE HAVE THE ADVANTAGE OF A HUGE BASE OF 50 YEARS OF SUPPORT FROM PEOPLE WHO HAVE BEEN COMING IN FOR A LONG TIME."

But the arts crowd is only part of the Black Forest's decades-long success story. Erica notes that people who lived in the neighborhood in years past tend to stop by the restaurant to say hello and gain a frame of reference for how much things have really changed. "It's a pretty big part of our business, the loyalty factor.

I don't know that a restaurant that opens today can develop that. We have the advantage of a huge base of 50 years of support from people who have been coming in for a long time."

As long as the Black Forest Inn stands, the history of Eat Street and the uncountable stories of the neighborhood and its characters will be available to anyone who strolls in to savor them — along with some of the best German food this side of the Rhine.

Dipping Sauce		Yields
Prep: 15 min.	Total: 24 hrs.	2 cups

BLACK FOREST INN

Bavarian Sweet Mustard

INGREDIENTS

3/4 cup ground yellow mustard seed

1/3 cup crushed brown mustard seed

1/2 cup firmly packed brown sugar

1/2 cup dark beer

1/4 cup cider vinegar

1/4 cup (scant) water

DIRECTIONS

Grind the yellow mustard seed, using a mortar and pestle or a burr-style coffee grinder.

Combine the ground yellow and brown mustard seed with the brown sugar in a bowl. In a stockpot, combine the vinegar, beer and water. Bring to a boil.

Combine the wet and dry ingredients, and set aside. Cover the mixture, and let ripen at room temperature for 24 hours (or longer, if you prefer a milder flavor).

Once you've mastered this recipe, horseradish or orange peel can be added to create different varieties.

Side Dish	Serves 6
Total time: 45 min.	veggie V

BLACK FOREST INN

Red Cabbage

INGREDIENTS

3/4 cup plus 2 tablespoons red wine vinegar

1 1/2 cups applesauce

1/2 cup plus 2 tablespoons sugar

1/2 teaspoon ground clove

1 bay leaf

4 1/2 teaspoons salt

1/2 teaspoon ground pepper

3/4 cup apple cider

2 1/2 pounds cored and sliced red cabbage

3 cups diced onion

DIRECTIONS

Combine vinegar, applesauce, sugar, cloves, bay leaf, apple cider, salt and pepper in a large cooking pot and bring to a boil over medium heat. Mix well, cooking for 10 minutes.

Mix in the cabbage and onion. Cook approximately 10–12 minutes, until cabbage is soft but still a little crunchy. Remove the bay leaves and season to taste.

Serve warm.

BLACK FOREST INN

Potato Salad

INGREDIENTS

4 ounces bacon

1 pound cooked red potatoes
(Yukon Golds are okay as well)

2 ounces (1/2 cup) diced fresh onion

3 tablespoons cider vinegar

1/2 teaspoon salt

1 generous pinch of black pepper

3 tablespoons chicken stock (or water)

DIRECTIONS

Sauté the bacon until thoroughly cooked but barely crisp, and remove from heat. Set bacon aside on a paper towel, leaving the bacon fat in the sauté pan. Slice into quarter-inch pieces once cool enough to handle, and return to the warm pan.

Bring the chicken stock (or water) to a boil. Reduce to low heat and leave covered.

In a large stockpot, steam the potatoes skin-on for 12 to 15 minutes, depending on size. When done, potatoes should be easy to break apart with a fork. Peel and slice the potatoes ¼ inch thick. Place in a large mixing bowl and cover to keep warm.

Add the bacon (with the fat), onions, vinegar, salt and pepper and enough of the liquid for a moist but not sloppy potato salad. Season to taste, and add liquid if preferred.

Serve warm or cold.

Side Dish	Serves 4-6
Total time: 45 min.	veggie V

EVERY DAY A

Báhn Mì

SINCE THE LATE 1970S, THE TWIN CITIES AREA HAS HOSTED ONE OF THE LARGER VIETNAMESE ENCLAVES IN AMERICA, WITH JUST ONE OF THE WONDERFUL RESULTS BEING THAT OUR FOOD SCENE HAS LONG BEEN DOTTED WITH VIETNAMESE RESTAURANTS.

A colonial mash-up of French and Vietnamese ingredients, bánh mì has become a global sandwich sensation in recent years. Inside a crusty baguette, mayonnaise and paté come together with sweet and crunchy pickled veggies, jalapeño, cucumber, and fresh cilantro atop layers of chả lụa (Vietnamese ham) and roast pork. The end result is a pitch-perfect balance of flavor, texture, and portability. On Nicollet, different riffs on the traditional pork-based mainstay perform the push-pull of the local and the global, with customizable versions and even vegan options on the menu.

In the greater Eat Street area, there are over a half-dozen Vietnamese restaurants, and almost all of them serve bánh mì. Here are some of the tastiest highlights.

N

Pho Hoa

Jasmine
DELI

Lu's
SANDWICHES

My Huong
KITCHEN

Quang
RESTAURANT

Pho Tau Bay

S

1

LU'S SANDWICHES

2624 Nicollet Avenue

Lu's brings an unmatched sauciness to the bánh mì game of Eat Street. Housemade mayo and paté that carries the tangy acidity of mustard give their bánh mì rich, intense flavor. And the baguette is second to none, crusty and soft. Open seven days a week.

2

JASMINE DELI

2532 Nicollet Avenue

Jasmine's savory and aromatic roast pork is at the heart of what makes their sandwiches great, but their yeasty bread and ultra-fresh cucumber and cilantro are also key parts of the equation. Closed Mondays.

3

QUANG

2719 Nicollet Avenue

Quang puts a strong emphasis on its chả lụa, and rightly so. With a combination of spice and sweetness on soft bread, with a little jalapeño bite, it's a unique and delicious take on the bánh mì. Closed Tuesdays.

4 PHO HOA

2450 Nicollet Avenue

Carrot, cucumber, and fish sauce are the first flavors you taste at Pho Hoa, followed by peanut and herbs from the meat and paté, all on the softest, chewiest bread on Eat Street. Open seven days a week.

5 PHO TAU BAY

2837 Nicollet Avenue

This is a bánh mì not for the faint of heart: lots of pepper and jalapeño are complemented by the generous portions of chả lụa on this sandwich. Closed Wednesdays.

6 MY HUONG

2718 Nicollet Avenue

My Huong's bánh mì is all about texture — crisp on the outside, soft in the middle. And there's so much going on in between — a slightly sweet mayo and plenty of cilantro and carrots. So satisfying. Closed Mondays.

NICOLLET
2507

Main Dishes

Fried Wild Rice with Chicken

Porcini Veggie Burger

Enchiladas Verdes

Green Curry with Chicken

Larb Salad

Chicken Pot Pie

Rainbow Chinese

2739 Nicollet Avenue

Tammy Wong is the heart and soul of Rainbow Chinese, a restaurant that, when it opened in 1987, was one of the first in Minneapolis to start steering its customers away from gloppy and cloying Americanized versions of Chinese cuisine and toward more authentic dishes. Although she wouldn't say so, Tammy is a pillar of the food and restaurant community in the Twin Cities, cited by chefs across generations who have worked with her, admired her passion, or simply love her food.

Tammy began cooking at five years of age as a child of ethnic Chinese parents growing up in Vietnam, helping her grandmother roll tamarind candies and cook rice over an open fire. She moved to Minneapolis in 1983 and worked at a number of Asian restaurants before opening Rainbow. The accolades have poured in ever since, and Rainbow Chinese is still considered a go-to spot for some of the freshest and most authentic Chinese in town.

> "WE DON'T HAVE CHINATOWN OR JAPANTOWN IN MINNEAPOLIS, BUT WE HAVE INTERNATIONAL EAT STREET! IT MAKES MINNEAPOLIS UNIQUE."

As a business owner and resident for the past 30 years, Tammy loves the neighborhood she's a part of, and has seen a lot of positive changes over the years.

"It used to be a really rough neighborhood, and people wouldn't want to come here," she says. "It's better these days. I really appreciate all the small businesses — myself, Quang, all the others — we stick around, you become a family, then more people come into the neighborhood... we don't have Chinatown or Japantown in Minneapolis, but we have international Eat Street! It makes Minneapolis unique."

Staying busy and prolific is what Tammy seems to do best — she has been a fixture at the Minneapolis Farmer's Market for years now, doing cooking demos, selling some of her creations, preserving and pickling vegetables, and connecting with farmers and others in the food community to keep learning and growing. Like Rainbow and Eat Street itself, she shows no signs of stopping — or even slowing down.

Main Dish	
Total time: 45 min. + overnight cooling	Serves 4-6

Fried Wild Rice with Chicken

INGREDIENTS

1/2 pound wild rice

2 cups water

1 tablespoon chicken stock

2 chicken breasts

1/2 small onion, diced

2 cloves of garlic, minced

3 eggs, lightly beaten

3 stalks of green onion, sliced

1 cup bean sprouts (optional)

2 tablespoons soy sauce

1 tablespoon sesame oil

3 tablespoons vegetable oil

DIRECTIONS

Preparation

The night before, rinse the wild rice thoroughly. Place in a saucepan with the water and chicken stock, and bring to a boil. Once boiling, turn the heat down to low and cover. Cook rice for a half hour or until the water is absorbed. After removing from the heat, fluff the rice with a fork.

While the rice is cooking, add 1 tablespoon of the vegetable oil to a sauté pan and heat over medium/high heat. Add the chicken breasts and sear until nicely browned, 3–4 minutes; flip and repeat on the other side. Cool the rice and chicken over night in the refrigerator.

Assembly

Have all of the ingredients prepared and close at hand: chop the chicken into small cubes. Scramble the eggs in a small sauté pan or wok, and set aside. Use a fork to break up any clumps that may have formed in the rice overnight. Slice the green onion; rinse and drain the bean sprouts.

Heat the remaining 2 tablespoons of vegetable oil in a wok or large sauté pan over high heat. Add the onions and garlic and cook, stirring constantly, until the onions become translucent, 1 to 2 minutes. Add the chicken and rice and continue to cook, stirring constantly for 5 to 7 more minutes.

Add the egg, green onion, bean sprouts (if using), sesame oil, and soy sauce. Cook, stirring vigorously, until everything is well incorporated. Serve and enjoy.

Icehouse

2528 Nicollet Avenue

Like many a great idea, Icehouse was conceived over drinks at a favorite bar of co-owners Matt Bickford and Brian Liebeck. Meeting every Monday for JT's Jazz Implosion at the Clown Lounge in the basement of Saint Paul's Turf Club, the initial vision was a means to create several things at once: their own, intimate listening room environment for the music they loved, new chapters in their careers, and (of course) a unique bar program.

Icehouse marked a return of music to Nicollet Avenue, which was once home to the Artists' Quarter, a legendary jazz club that moved to Saint Paul in the mid-1990s. "We didn't realize there was so much passion for live music in the neighborhood that wasn't being answered," Bickford recalls. The neighborhood — and really, much of south Minneapolis — responded quickly and enthusiastically to Icehouse, now in its fourth year on Nicollet.

But just as Eat Street has grown more diverse since the 90s, the demand for music in the neighborhood has become more eclectic. In addition to rebooting JT's Jazz Implosion on Monday nights, Liebeck reflects how "having people like [local rapper] Lizzo in the neighborhood, having [veteran sound engineer] Jay Pearlman work with us — all those natural interests that arose really helped us." Nowadays, Icehouse brings an array of music to Nicollet, from guitar virtuoso Tim Sparks at brunch to the avant-drone collective Marijuana Death Squads in the earliest hours of the morning.

"WE DIDN'T REALIZE THERE WAS SO MUCH PASSION FOR LIVE MUSIC IN THE NEIGHBORHOOD THAT WASN'T BEING ANSWERED,"

That's not to say food is an afterthought at Icehouse — if anything, the bar's approach to food employs all the skills of great musicianship. It listens to the other players. It responds to its audience without pandering to it. And when the whole ensemble gives it a few measures to solo, it slays. There's no blueprint for food at Icehouse, just execution of any idea at the highest level possible.

And that's the challenge Icehouse takes up: making itself more than what anyone could have conceived it to be — more than a music venue, more than a restaurant, more than a strong cocktail program. Thankfully, it's had a lot of help along the way. "Mia has been a huge supporter, even involving us in some of their events. MCAD did our original logo, too," says Liebeck, describing the broader artistic roots of the neighborhood that the bar has become an important part of.

ICEHOUSE

Porcini Veggie Burger

Main Dish	Serves
Active: 15 min.	6-8
Total: 60 min.	veggie V

Icehouse Executive Chef Matt Bickford explains, "It's important for us that the porcini burger isn't an afterthought, just a non-meat option; everything we do here we like to do at a high level. We're kind of fundamentally about elevating simple cuisine, and that's something that American cuisine lends itself to. The oats, the panko — they soak up the excess liquids to create flavor. It's about taking a series of techniques and stringing them together properly."

INGREDIENTS

5 yellow onions, diced

15 cloves garlic, minced

2 cups steel cut oats

2 sprigs thyme

1 cup dried porcini mushrooms

2 1/2 cups water

1 1/2 tablespoon salt

1/2 tablespoon pepper

1/2 cup chopped parsley

1 tablespoon tarragon

4 cups quick oats

1/2 cup panko breadcrumbs, plus more for coating

DIRECTIONS

Preparation

Soak the dried porcini mushrooms in hot water. Once they've rehydrated, drain them and reserve the soaking liquid. Roughly chop and set aside.

Combine the diced onion and 2 to 3 tablespoons butter in a sauté pan. Over medium heat, cook the onion until caramelized and golden brown.

Place the remaining onion, garlic, steel cut oats, salt, pepper, thyme, and water into a baking dish, and cover with aluminum foil. Place in a 300-degree oven for about 30 minutes, until oats are cooked and the water has evaporated.

In a large bowl, mix the cooked oats with quick oats, porcinis, panko, caramelized onion, and herbs. Continue to hand mix until fully incorporated. Salt to taste.

Assembly

Make 1-inch thick patties with the mixture, and coat with additional panko. Sauté the patties in oil or butter over medium heat until golden on the outside and warmed throughout.

Serve with your favorite burger toppings. Taleggio cheese, mustard, and caramelized onion are particularly nice.

Marissa's Supermarket & Bakery

2750 Nicollet Avenue

The scent of fresh tortillas is the first thing you'll notice at Marissa's — but it's only the beginning of the huge variety of smells, sights, and tastes at this supermarket, deli, and bakery that offers Mexican staples for cooking at home or eating on the spot.

Caesar Perez, the owner, was born in Morelos, Mexico. His father and grandfather were bakers, so he followed in the family footsteps. "I was born in a bakery," says Caesar. "Nobody taught me how to make the bread, because I had seen it done since I was walking. Later, they taught me a few things... down the road, I invented about 5 or 6 recipes of my own."

"I REALLY LOVE THE NEIGHBORHOOD — IT'S MY FAVORITE NEIGHBORHOOD IN THE CITY."

And that family tradition is being passed on to Araceli, Caesar's daughter. "Growing up, my dad would always want us to come here on the weekends. It was his way of spending time with us — in high school I worked at the cash register, and my older sister worked in the bakery... I went to school for business, came back, and started working with him full time."

Being present on Nicollet Avenue for over 20 years means that the Perez family has seen this neighborhood change at every turn over the years. "I was pretty little when my dad moved in," says Araceli. "It was a bad neighborhood — we always do Sunday dinners and since it's so easy on Eat Street, we'd go out to eat on Sunday nights — and a couple of times, our car got broken into, things like that. But now I really love the neighborhood — it's my favorite neighborhood in the city."

As the neighborhood changes, so does Marissa's — the Perez family has big plans to remodel and add on in the coming years. And with the fresh flavors of their Mexican heritage front and center, the sky, it seems, is the only limit.

SUPERMARKET
DELI
MARISSA'S

INSIDER TIP

To save time, buy a rotisserie chicken and shred the meat.

Main Dish	
Active: 15 min.	Serves 6-8
Total: 50-60 min.	

MARISSA'S SUPERMARKET & BAKERY

Enchiladas Verdes

There are three stages to making enchiladas verdes: cooking the chicken itself, making the sauce, and assembling the enchiladas. All the ingredients you need to make Araceli's enchiladas are available to purchase at Marissa's. The simple recipe was a favorite of hers growing up, which Araceli often made with her mom as a kid.

"IN THE U.S., MEXICAN FOOD IS VERY REGIONAL," SAYS ARACELI. "THIS IS MORE CENTRAL-NORTHERN — THE MAJORITY OF MEXICANS IN MINNESOTA ARE FROM MORELOS. EVERY TIME I MEET SOMEONE, WE HAVE A RELATIVE IN COMMON!"

INGREDIENTS

CHICKEN FILLING

2 pounds chicken breast

1/2 white onion, diced

2 garlic cloves

2 tablespoons salt

TOMATILLO SAUCE

3 pounds of tomatillos

3-4 serrano peppers

1/4 white onion

3 garlic cloves

DIRECTIONS

Chicken

Place the chicken breasts in a saucepan with onion, garlic, and salt. Add enough water to cover the ingredients. Bring the water to a boil, and then reduce to medium heat. Cover and let simmer until chicken is cooked, approximately 15–20 minutes.

Remove the chicken and set aside to cool. Reserve a half cup of cooking liquid. Once the chicken has cooled, shred the meat with two forks.

Alternatively, you can skip this step all together and buy a rotisserie chicken and shred the meat — just don't use the skin. Likewise, if you prefer another meat altogether, pulled pork or beef will excel in this dish.

Tomatillo Sauce

Remove the husks from the tomatillos; core the serrano peppers and discard the seeds.

In a saucepan, cover the tomatillos and serrano peppers with water and bring to a boil. Once boiling, reduce to medium heat and cook until tender, about 10–15 min. Drain the tomatillos and peppers, combine with the onion and garlic in a blender, and process until a smooth sauce forms.

Return the sauce to the saucepan, stirring regularly over medium heat until the sauce begins to bubble; reduce the heat to low and cook until the sauce starts to thicken. Add salt to taste, approximately 1 tablespoon. If the sauce thickens too much, add in some of the chicken cooking liquid you've reserved.

ENCHILADAS

1/2 cup canola oil

Corn tortillas

TOPPINGS

Crema Mexicana

Crumbled queso fresco

1 thinly sliced white onion

Enchiladas

Heat the oil in a frying pan over medium heat. Using tongs, quickly pass each tortilla through the oil until softened, then set to rest on a paper towel.

Using your fingers or tongs, quickly drag each tortilla through the warm sauce, and place on a baking dish. Fill the tortilla with two spoonfuls of chicken, roll the tortilla around it, and begin to line up the enchiladas in a row. Repeat until your baking dish is full.

Cover the enchiladas with the remaining sauce and bake in a preheated oven at 350 degrees for 10 minutes.

Toppings

Top with crema Mexicana, crumbled queso fresco, and thinly sliced white onions. Additional toppings such as lettuce, tomatoes, and avocado take this to the next level.

Khunnai Thai Cuisine

2523 Nicollet Avenue

If there's one constant theme on Eat Street, it's change. Even among the titans of the neighborhood, like the Black Forest Inn or Rainbow Chinese, evolution happens — every business that opens or closes will have a ripple effect of some kind; no restaurant is an island. It's a symbiotic community.

"IN THAILAND, MY AUNT LIVED NEAR US, AND SHE HAD A RESTAURANT. I HELPED OUT AS A LITTLE KID. AT KHUNNAI, WE'LL HAVE SOME OF THE SAME DISHES FROM HER RECIPES."

And so it's fitting that one of Eat Street's Thai gems, Krung Thep Thai, is evolving at this very moment. Sue Yotharak operated Krung Thep Thai on Eat Street for about five years, serving up authentic and deeply spiced takes on classic Thai dishes that aren't often found in other Midwestern Thai restaurants. Recently, however, a whole new opportunity presented itself.

"The owner [of Krung Thep] made plans to retire," says Sue. "We talked, and I said OK — if you plan to close down, why don't I just take over?"

Khunnai Thai Cuisine is Sue's new venture — loosely translated, Khunnai refers to an upper-class lady. Sue is most definitely a classy lady — and she intends to extend that energy into the new concept.

Originally from southern Thailand, Sue is connecting with her roots via the new approach at Khunnai. "In Thailand, my aunt lived near us, and she had a restaurant. I helped out as a little kid. At Khunnai, we'll have some of the same dishes from her recipes."

A big point of pride for Sue is that during her tenure operating Krung Thep, there has been zero turnover in staff, both in the kitchen and on the floor. This is unheard of in the industry — and every single employee is coming along for the Khunnai ride.

Sue will retain and refine most of the menu items people love at Krung Thep as she begins to develop and deploy her own recipes. She's most excited about her green curry — a version of which she's shared here (minus a few secret ingredients in the family recipe).

Green Curry with Chicken

(KANG KEA WAN KAI)

INGREDIENTS

1/4 cup of green curry paste

1 pound of chicken breast cut in bite-sized cubes

1 14-oz. can of coconut milk

1/2 cup of chicken stock or water

2 teaspoons of plum sugar (brown sugar is ok as a substitute, but less fragrant and sweeter)

3 tablespoons of fish sauce

1/4 cup Thai basil leaves

4 kaffir lime leaves

1 pound Thai eggplants, quartered

1 red bell pepper, sliced

4 cups steamed jasmine rice, for serving

DIRECTIONS

Over medium heat, bring ½ cup of coconut milk (use the thick cream off the top) to a boil in a pot, stirring often for 3 to 5 minutes. Add green curry paste; continue to cook and stir until the mixture becomes uniform in color and fragrant.

Add the chicken and stir for 1 to 2 minutes. Add the fish sauce and sugar, and continue to stir. Add the eggplant and red bell pepper, as well as the remaining coconut milk and chicken stock. Cook over medium heat until the chicken is cooked through and eggplant is tender.

Add kaffir lime leaves and Thai basil. Bring to a boil for one to two minutes. Remove from heat and salt to taste.

Transfer to a large serving bowl, and enjoy with steamed jasmine rice.

Main Dish

Total time: 45 min.

Serves

4

Main Dish

Total time: 30 min.

Serves 4

KHUNNAI THAI CUISINE

Larb Salad

INGREDIENTS

1 pound ground pork, chicken, mock duck, or tofu

2 tablespoons fresh mint leaves

3 tablespoons lime juice

2 tablespoons fish sauce

1/2 tablespoons sugar

2 tablespoons toasted rice powder

3 tablespoons finely chopped g reen onion

2 tablespoons coarsely chopped cilantro

1 tablespoon coarsely ground dried red chili

1/2 cup coarsely chopped shallot

1 cup water (or chicken stock)

Cabbage, cut into 2-inch wedges

1 cucumber, sliced

2 tomatoes, sliced

4 cups of sticky rice or steamed jasmine rice, for serving

DIRECTIONS

Heat the water in a saucepan or small pot. Add ground meat and cook for 2 minutes, tossing often to break up the meat. When cooked, remove the pan from the heat and drain the water.

Transfer the cooked meat to a medium bowl. Add the lime juice, fish sauce, rice powder, chili, and sugar and mix well. Add the shallot, spring onion, cilantro, and most of the mint leaves, reserving a few for a garnish. Stir to combine everything well.

Before serving, garnish the serving dish with the cabbage, cucumber, tomatoes, and mint. Enjoy with a side of sticky rice or steamed jasmine rice.

The Copper Hen

2515 Nicollet Avenue

If you lived on a farm, what would you want to eat when you returned to the farmhouse after a long day of backbreaking labor?

The answer is on the menu at The Copper Hen Cakery & Kitchen. From rich, pastry-topped chicken pot pie to creamy baked mac and cheese, The Copper Hen serves up comfort food made from scratch using locally-sourced ingredients. The passion for doing things the old-fashioned way, it seems, is baked directly into Danielle and Chris Bjorling's personal philosophies.

Danielle grew up with a lot of love for homemade food, and a particular passion for baking and cake decorating. After working at a few bakeries, she began catering weddings on the side. But as word-of-mouth grew, she found herself baking more cupcakes than her 900-square-foot apartment could handle. "So, we decided to take the leap," says Danielle. "Chris has always had an entrepreneurial spirit. We didn't have much experience, and we were very naïve — so we made the perfect team to pull it off!"

"WE DIDN'T HAVE MUCH EXPERIENCE, AND WE WERE VERY NAÏVE — SO WE MADE THE PERFECT TEAM TO PULL IT OFF!"

Eat Street had always been a haunt for the pair, who would often grab coffee at Spyhouse and eat in the neighborhood. When they happened upon the Edison building on 25th and Nicollet, the building was a wreck, "but it was the perfect space, and the perfect area," says Danielle.

As if to further proof of their love for the neighborhood, Danielle and Chris make their home in the apartment above the restaurant. They moved in just as they began construction on The Copper Hen, walking downstairs to grind out long days of hard work, and then eating takeout from their favorite neighborhood spots. Consciously or not, they seemed to be embodying the modern, urban version of the

quaint farmhouse vision they set forth for the restaurant — and as such, they have no shortage of recommendations in the area.

"I love the Christo's Greek salad," says Danielle. "Black Sheep's house salad and meatball pizza are great, and we go to Pho 79 for pho. Kung Fu Noodle has the best steamed buns on the street. Quang for pad Thai. After a busy day, the late-night chicken quesadilla from Pancho Villa. The fermented veggie jar at Icehouse is amazing, too."

INSIDER TIP

The crust benefits from being partially baked separately on a sheet pan at 350-degrees for 10–12 minutes. The dough should be lightly golden brown, and no longer translucent in the middle.

Main Dish	
Total time: 2 1/2 hrs.	Serves 8-12

THE COPPER HEN

Chicken Pot Pie

The Copper Hen's take on this Midwestern classic absolutely nails the best elements of this beloved classic. It embodies all that's great about scratch cooking, striking a unique balance with flavorful chicken, standout gravy, and the tender-yet-firm fresh vegetables which bring a natural sweetness. "It's a great fall and winter cozy Sunday afternoon dish," says Danielle. "Take the time to cook all day, and let the fragrance fill the house. It's mainly just about invoking that cozy feel and having a slow, long day."

There are several steps to this recipe, and cooks will do well to review and plan ahead. You can use a rotisserie chicken from the store to save time.

INGREDIENTS

CHICKEN

1 whole chicken

2 carrots, peeled and roughly chopped

3 stalks of celery, roughly chopped

2 onions, roughly chopped

1 bay leaf

1 tablespoon whole peppercorns

POT PIE MIXTURE

3 medium carrots, diced

2 medium potatoes, diced

4 stalks of celery, diced

1/4 cup butter

1/4 cup flour

1/2 teaspoon thyme

2 tablespoons parsley

1 cup heavy cream

PIE DOUGH

4 1/2 cups flour

1 1/2 teaspoons salt

1 3/4 cups unsalted butter (3 1/2 sticks)

1 1/4 cups water

FINAL ASSEMBLY

2 onions, diced

1/2 cup frozen peas

DIRECTIONS

Chicken

Place the whole chicken and broth ingredients in large stockpot. Cover with water and bring to a boil. Reduce to a simmer and let cook for 2 hours.

Remove chicken from broth and set aside to cool. Strain the chicken broth and reserve the liquid.

Once cooled, cut the chicken into pieces, removing the skin. Pull the meat from the bones and cut into half-inch cubes.

Pie Dough

Combine flour and salt. Remove butter from refrigerator, and cut pea-sized chunks of butter into the mixture. Add water slowly while stirring, using only enough water for dough to pull together. Refrigerate the dough mixture while preparing the other pie components.

Pot Pie Mixture

Toss potatoes, carrots and celery with oil and roast in a 425-degree oven for 10 minutes.

Final Assembly

Sauté the onions in butter until translucent. Whisk in flour and cook your roux for one minute on medium low heat. Stir regularly to avoid burning the flour. Add the heavy cream and 1½ cups of chicken broth to the roux and stir.

Once the mixture has begun to simmer, add two cups of the chicken, roasted vegetables and peas. Season with salt and pepper to taste, and add the parsley and thyme. Add additional stock and cream if needed.

Place the mixture in a 9-inch by 2-inch (2 quart) pie pan and top with crust. A 9-inch square pan can be used as well — glass or ceramic is preferred.

Bake for 20 minutes at 425-degrees or until the filling is hot and bubbly, and the top crust is fully baked.

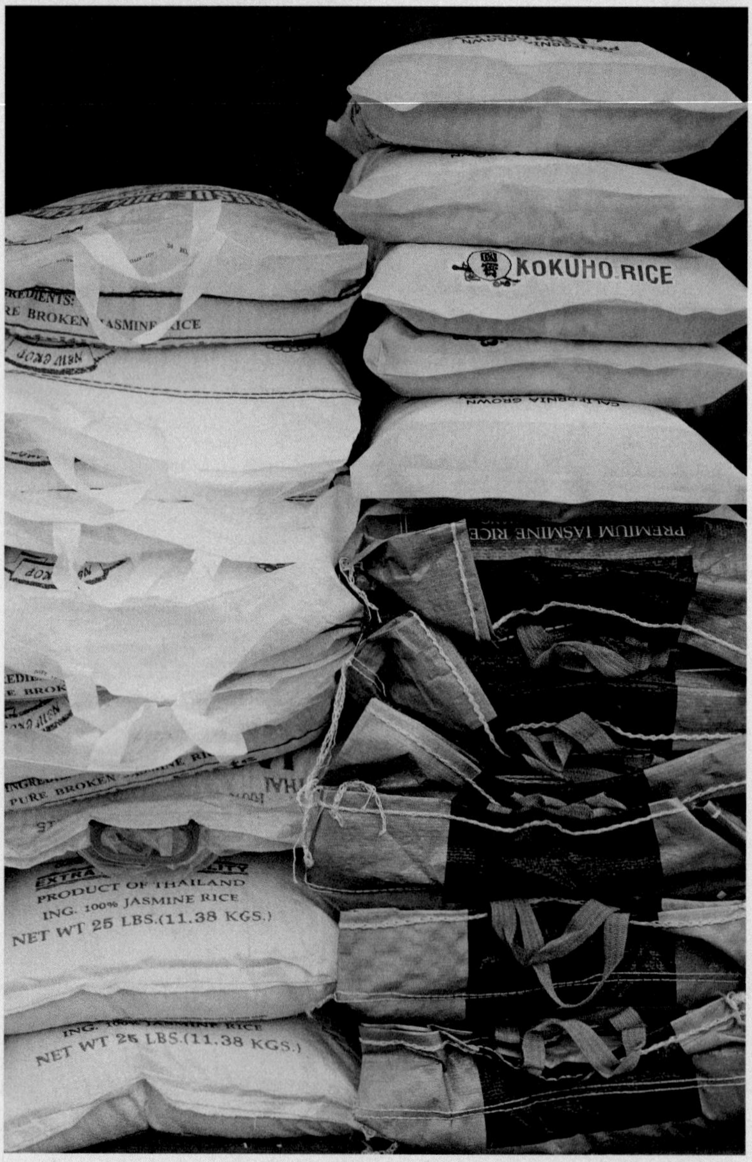
KOKUHO RICE
PURE BROKEN JASMINE RICE
PRODUCT OF THAILAND
ING. 100% JASMINE RICE
NET WT 25 LBS.(11.38 KGS.)
NET WT 25 LBS.(11.38 KGS.)

Treats

Greater Goods

2515 Nicollet Avenue

City of Lakes
$24
WHITTIER
$24
Herbs & Spices
$45
$45
National Parks of the United States of America
$45
GRAB A SEAT, GRAB A PEN, and WRITE AWHILE.
$18
Tapercandle

It's not just restaurants that give Eat Street its character — the shops and businesses that line the street and give those restaurants custom, as well as providing the neighborhood with the services it needs, are just as much a part of the community.

And Greater Goods, a gift and stationery shop with a mission to give back, is a great example of how businesses can support each other and their neighborhood. Lauren and Joel Grynewski, Greater Goods' owners, landed in their Nicollet Avenue storefront after years in advertising. The shop started out in a warehouse as a mail-order business, but they realized they wanted a storefront where they could interact with people and provide more to their community.

With that openness to the outside world as part of their mission, Greater Goods gives 5% of their sales every year to a local organization. In the past, they've helped provide scholarships to low-income kids and teens participating in the summer youth art program at the Minneapolis College of Art and Design; last year's donation went to St. Stephen's Human Services — an organization in the neighborhood that's working to end homelessness across Minneapolis. In 2016, they'll help support the Walk-In Counseling Center, which provides free, anonymous mental health counseling to anyone who walks through its doors.

> **"THERE'S A LOT OF CROSS-POLLINATION. SPYHOUSE, THE COPPER HEN, WEDGE TABLE — WE ALL HAVE EMPLOYEES WE SHARE FROM TIME TO TIME,"**

But in another sense, they got more than they bargained for by opening their doors on Nicollet. "There's a lot of cross-pollination," Lauren says. "Spyhouse, The Copper Hen, Wedge Table — we all have employees we share from time to time," creating the unintended benefit of familiar faces that help personify the neighborhood.

And, with all that restaurant experience coming in and out of the store, they're qualified to share a recipe, too.

Beverage

Total time: 5 min.

Yields 1

GREATER GOODS

Strawberry Basil Fields Forever

YOU WILL NEED

2 ounces gin
(preferably Nolet or Leopold Bros.)

1 tablespoon Red Camper Strawberry Limoncello jam (or your favorite strawberry jam)

A few sprigs of fresh basil

3/4 ounces of fresh lemon or lime juice

Ice

A cocktail shaker

A muddler

DIRECTIONS

Pour your gin into the shaker, strip the best 4–5 leaves off the stems of the basil and muddle them together.

Add the jam and lemon or lime juice to the shaker, and then fill with ice. Shake briefly and vigorously. Strain with a fine strainer into the cocktail glass. Garnish with fresh basil.

Eat Street Social

18 W. 26th Street

Eat Street Social is as much a way of life as it is a place to gather your best friends around some of the best cocktails in the city. "The social principle is to be guest-first, but it's about building that culture within the staff so that they can extend that to the guest," owner Sam Bonin explains.

An iteration of their original Northeast Social concept on the other side of downtown Minneapolis, Eat Street Social's charter has always been one of inclusivity. For Sam, co-owner Joe Wagner, and bar manager Keith Werner, an expanding definition of service never goes out of style. "You can get the right ingredients anywhere now," Sam explains. "What's really unique about the neighborhood is how it allows us as a business to really open up."

Beyond a come-one-come-all approach, Eat Street Social casts a wide net to its peers — the restaurant has hosted over 20 pop-up events with different artisanal food and beverage makers. And developing talent within the restaurant helps keep familiar faces around. "It's really fulfilling for us as owners, investing in our employees through things like tasting experiences and education," says Sam, reflecting on how to ensure the guest comes first in what can often be a transient profession.

Eat Street Social aspires to a uniquely bohemian feel that's not easy to come by, something spontaneous but with a passion for detail. In the late afternoon, when light pours in through the southern windows, and the staff might outnumber guests, the hustle and chatter throughout the bar conveys the ceremony of a big family gathering rather than the business of coworkers preparing for dinner service. It's a buzz of warmth and possibility that carries on and amplifies itself into the wee hours of the night.

"WHAT'S REALLY UNIQUE ABOUT THE NEIGHBORHOOD IS HOW IT ALLOWS US AS A BUSINESS TO REALLY OPEN UP."

EAT STREET
SOCIAL

Beverage	Serves enough for a small party	Approx. 20 drinks
Total time: 30 min.		

EAT STREET SOCIAL

Mulled Wine

DIRECTIONS

Bring the apple cider, orange juice, and water to a simmer. Add the spice mix and let simmer, continuing to whisk. Add the burgundy wine, honey, and sugar. Strain into a serving vessel and add the apple brandy. Serve warm.

INGREDIENTS

6 1/4 cups burgundy wine (approx. two 750 ml bottles)

1 1/4 cups apple brandy (preferably Copper & Kings)

1 cup apple cider

1/2 cup orange juice

1 cup honey

1/4 cup granulated sugar

1 cup water

SPICE MIX

5 cinnamon sticks

12 cloves

25 allspice berries

1 half nutmeg, grated

Peel of 1 orange

1/2 teaspoons vanilla extract

1/4 cup fresh chopped ginger

1/2 cup raisins

1/4 cup almonds

2 1/2 teaspoon cocoa powder

4 sprigs fresh sage

EAT STREET SOCIAL

Summer Sangria

INGREDIENTS

3/4 cup burgundy wine

5 1/2 cups dry white wine
(you'll need two 750ml bottles)

2 tablespoons Luxardo
Maraschino cherries

1/2 cup Myer's dark rum

3/4 cup white rum

1/2 cup vodka

1/4 cup pineapple juice

Juice of one half lime

1/4 cup orange juice

1 cup Summer Slurry (see below)

SUMMER SLURRY

1 nutmeg, whole

4 cinnamon sticks

1/4 cup ginger, thinly sliced

4 star anise

2 1/2 tablespoons grenadine

2 1/4 teaspoons honey

1 1/4 cup sugar

1 1/4 cup water

Beverage	Serves enough for a small party	Approx. 20 drinks
Total time: 40 min.		

DIRECTIONS

First make the Summer Slurry by bringing water to a simmer, and adding the dry spices and ginger. Let simmer over low heat for 12 minutes. Remove from heat, cover and leave for 6 minutes, then stir for thirty seconds and strain. Add the sugar, continuing to stir. Once the sugar has dissolved, add the honey and grenadine. Set aside.

In a punch bowl or large pitcher mix the burgundy wine, white wine, dark rum, white rum, vodka, pineapple, lime and orange juices. Add 1 cup of Summer Slurry. Serve chilled with Maraschino cherries.

Spyhouse Coffee

2451 Nicollet Avenue

Opened in 2000 by Christian Johnson, Spyhouse has stood on the corner of 25th and Nicollet Avenue for 16 years. During that time, it has evolved from Christian's original vision as an arts-centered social house into one of the premier coffee roasters in Minneapolis. Today, Spyhouse exists in four locations around Minneapolis, and with each new iteration, Christian pushes his design-forward aesthetic a bit further, along with the excellence of his coffee.

"I WENT TO CAFFETTO TO KEEP WARM, AND STUDIED THERE THROUGH MY WHOLE COLLEGE CAREER. THAT'S HOW I GOT INTO COFFEE."

Yet the Eat Street location — where it all began — remains special. And you might say that opening his own café was born out of a uniquely Minnesotan necessity: when Christian moved to Minneapolis in 1993, he rented an apartment with no heat, which led him to spend lots of time at local cafés just to stay sane during the deep freeze of winter. The rest, as they say, is history. "I went to Caffetto [a café on Lyndale Avenue] to keep warm, and studied there through my whole college career," says Christian. "That's how I got into coffee."

In the beginning, Spyhouse focused less on coffee, and more on atmosphere. The space was filled with vintage furniture, giving it a distinctly bohemian vibe. But around 2010, the café became sleeker and more modern, with clean lines, dark wood, and an overall aesthetic that hewed closer to Christian's design sensibilities. "The way this store is now is the best I can do in terms of design without gutting it — when we opened, we didn't know anything about this stuff."

At the same time, the coffee at Spyhouse made a quantum leap in quality and focus as Spyhouse began working with small specialty roasters, creating exacting cups that highlighted a particular bean's qualities. Soon they began roasting their own, hiring a dedicated roaster to handle the prized 1950s-era roasting machine in their Northeast Minneapolis location. Nowadays, Spyhouse's coffee is sold at businesses up and down the street and across Minneapolis, and also provides the caffeinated fuel for many of the neighborhood's employees and residents.

Beverage	Yields
Total time: 10 min.	2 cups

SPYHOUSE COFFEE

Chemex Brewed Coffee

YOU WILL NEED

6-cup Chemex coffeemaker

Chemex filter

Kitchen Scale

40 grams (roughly 1 1/3 cups) Spyhouse coffee, ground

650 milliliters (roughly 2 3/4 cups) hot water
+ extra for rinsing the filter

"THE CHEMEX IS GREAT IF YOU'RE BREWING FOR TWO OR MORE PEOPLE. CLASSIC 1940S DESIGN — IT'S IN THE MOMA.'

1

Fold your Chemex filter.

2

Place the filter in the brewer with the 3 layer side facing the spout. Rinse the filter by pouring hot water over the entire filter and discarding the rinse water. Add coffee to filter and shake lightly to level the bed of grounds.

INSIDER TIP

Grinding and water temperature are the two most important variables — you want a burr grinder instead of a blade grinder and you want the water hot enough for extraction, but not at boiling point.

3

Pour water in four cycles at the following times (4 minutes and 30 seconds total):

0:00 Pour 80 milliliters (⅓ cup) of water evenly over the grounds and allow to saturate.

0:45 Slowly bring the total water volume to 350 milliliters (1 ½ cups)

2:00 Slowly bring the total water volume to 500 milliliters (2 cups)

3:00 Slowly bring the total water volume to 650 milliliters (2 ¾ cups)

The drawdown should slow to drips at approximately 4:30.

4

Serve in two mugs, and enjoy!

Glam Doll Donuts

2605 Nicollet Avenue

In February of 2013, Glam Doll hit the Minneapolis dining scene with a tidal wave of creative donuts. Along with a saucy wink from their brand's signature pinup girl, owners Arwyn Birch and Teresa Fox — best friends since age ten — distilled their shared love of art, music, food, and vintage design into donuts that capture the spirit of playfulness at the heart of their business.

Right around the corner from Eat Street veteran the Black Forest Inn (and sharing part of its kitchen), Glam Doll opened on what was, at the time, a relatively quiet stretch of real estate just south of 26th street — and not everyone thought their concept would be a hit. "When we signed the lease," says Arwyn, "our landlord Erich said to us, 'I don't get it, but good luck, kid!'"

Yet from the moment they opened their doors, Arwyn and Teresa have had the envious problem of more demand than they can keep up with. Today, they're on the cusp of opening a second location in Northeast Minneapolis — impressive for a business that was created from scratch just three short years ago.

Being slammed with business right out of the gate created huge staffing challenges for Glam Doll. "We didn't have time to hire people," says Arwyn. "Both of us were working

21 hours a day, and I lost like 30 pounds — best diet ever! No sleep. That's always been the challenge — keeping good people. Now, we have an awesome core of like 6 people who really get it — it's not just us anymore. We have solid values now, four years into it, and goals, and our whole team reflects all that now. So you attract those people — misfit kids, weirdoes... but we're all good people!"

"[EAT STREET] IS MOSTLY EITHER IMMIGRANT OR FEMALE BUSINESS OWNERS, WHICH IS PRETTY AWESOME,"

And being on Eat Street is part of the charm and character that makes Glam Doll who they are.

"It's all local businesses," says Teresa. "There's MCAD, so you get young students, but then there's more sophisticated food for adults, too. There are options for everyone."

"And it's mostly either immigrant or female business owners, which is pretty awesome," Arwyn adds.

GLAM DOLL DONUTS

Best Pumpkin Pie in the World!

Pumpkin pie is not a donut, but Glam Doll's recipe is enough to make you forget that. "You just can't really make donuts at home. It sucks," says Teresa. "And no one makes pumpkin pie with real pumpkins anymore!" says Arwyn. "We've always had a connection with Teresa's grandmother's cooking and recipes for our icings and frostings. We got these pie pumpkins in Sanborn, MN one year and decided to make pumpkin pies out of them."

When it comes to the crust, however, the Glam Doll ladies aren't purists. "Screw the crust from scratch — use the Pillsbury ones. It's totally fine to get prepared crust." Use the time you save to make real whipped cream from scratch.

INSIDER TIP

Skip making the crust from scatch and use the time you save to make homemade whipped cream.

Dessert	Serves 6-8
Total time: 2 hrs.	veggie V

INGREDIENTS

1 sugar pumpkin, approximately four pounds.

1 9-inch pie crust, store-bought or your favorite recipe

1/2 teaspoon ground ginger

1/2 teaspoon cinnamon

1 teaspoon salt

4 eggs

1 cup of honey (warmed up)

1/2 cup of whole milk

1 pint heavy whipping cream beat with an electric mixer until fluffy (optional)

DIRECTIONS

Preheat an oven to 325 degrees. Slice the pumpkin in half, scoop out and discard the seeds and guts. Place the pumpkin cut side down on a cake or sheet pan covered in foil. Bake until tender, approximately 45 minutes.

Scrape the pumpkin into the food processor and puree. Combine 2 cups of pureed pumpkin with milk, spices, salt, honey and eggs.

Pour into a 9-inch pie tin. Bake at 400 degrees for 50–60 minutes. As an optional garnish, top with homemade whipped cream.

The Bad Waitress

2 E 26th St.

The Bad Waitress gives Eat Street what every good neighborhood needs — an honest diner in the old-school American tradition that serves breakfast all day.

Holding down the northeast corner of 26th Street and Nicollet Avenue, The Bad Waitress moniker is an ironic wink at their counter-service sensibility. Grab a booth, a menu, write your own ticket with a pad and pencil, bring it to the counter to pay, and voila! The Bad Waitress more than makes up for its purposeful lack of table service with reliable plates that overflow with well executed classics. Benedicts, pancakes, scrambles, club sandwiches and more, in cozy vinyl booths with plenty of strong Spyhouse coffee.

"THE PEOPLE ARE THE BEST PART OF THIS PLACE. THE RELATIONSHIPS, THE FAMILY FEELING WITH STAFF, AND THE REGULARS,"

David Wiedmeyer, the kitchen manager, has been running the kitchen at The Bad Waitress since the year it opened, so he's seen Eat Street change over the years — for the better.

SOUTHWEST

"I remember going to Little T's [the well-known nickname for longstanding Mexican restaurant Little Tijuana's] when I was underage. It was pretty shady around here... I would park my car right here where The Bad Waitress now stands, to go to Little T's."

It's clear that the Eat Street neighborhood has achieved a just-right, Goldilocks-like balance point in recent years, retaining the things people love about the area while bringing in just enough new businesses and residents to keep it evolving.

"I like that it's an eclectic neighborhood," says David. "You've got the art school [MCAD], halfway houses, a cool mix of people here — I like it much more than if we were on Hennepin Avenue... If most of the indie places can stay in business, I think the neighborhood will keep its integrity," says David.

No matter how Eat Street changes over the coming decade, it's a safe bet that the Bad Waitress will always be here to serve up pancakes to those in need, at any time of day.

"The people are the best part of this place. The relationships, the family feeling with staff, and the regulars," says David. "The community here is really important."

The
WEIRDEST
visitor
the Earth
has ever
seen!
The MAN FROM
PLANET X
BULLETS WON'T KILL IT!
FLAMES CAN'T HURT IT!
NOTHING CAN STOP IT!
THE
SPIDER
WILL EAT YOU ALIVE!
secured by ADT

Wild Rice Cranberry Pancakes

Main Dish	Serves 4-6
Total time: 35 min.	veggie V

INGREDIENTS

1 cup cooked wild rice

1 cup cooked cranberries

1 cup rolled oats

3 cups buttermilk

2 eggs

2 cup all-purpose flour

2 tablespoons canola oil

2 teaspoons baking soda

1 teaspoon salt

2 tablespoons sugar

1/4 teaspoon cinnamon

1/4 teaspoon fresh ground ginger

4 tablespoons maple syrup

DIRECTIONS

Place the cranberries in a small saucepan and cover with water. Bring to a slow boil, adding liquid as needed to keep the cranberries from sticking to the bottom of the saucepan. Once they have begun to break down, lower the heat and reduce the remaining liquid.

Mix the dry and wet ingredients separately, and combine in a large mixing bowl. Add ½ cup wild rice and ½ cup cranberries to pancake batter.

Heat 1 tablespoon butter or vegetable oil in a skillet or griddle. As the fat begins to reach its smoke point, pour ½ cup pancake batter onto the hot surface, making 6-inch diameter pancakes; reduce heat to avoid burning, if needed. Once the pancakes have risen in the pan, flip and cook for another two or three minutes.

When ready to serve, top the pancakes with remaining wild rice and cranberries.

Special thanks to

EAT STREET CONTRIBUTORS

Yoni Reinharz & Tomme Beevas

Colin Cody

Carol Parpas

Kylene and Mel Guse

Erica & Joanne Chryst

Tammy Wong

Matt Bickford & Brian Liebeck

Araceli & Caesar Perez

Sue Yotharak

Danielle Bjorling

Lauren Grynewski

Sam Bonin & Keith Werner

Christian Johnson

Arwyn Birch & Teresa Fox

Mary Cohen & David Wiedmeyer

EDITORS

Claire Dawson

Katie Iwanin

Sarah Lansky

Rob White

AUTHORS

Pete Sieve

Robert Skoro

DESIGNERS

Rachel Hardacre

Natalie Heisterkamp

Missy Reinikainen

Lindsay St. Clair